To my parents
Thank you for everything.
I love you

ISBN: 1542933048

Copyright 2017 Kelly Airhart
All rights reserved. This book or portion of thereof may not be reproduced or used in any manner without the express written permission of the author except for the use of brief quotations in a book review

The Visitor

How do you say it,
that town where you live?
What's in this food?
I've never heard of it!
What do you do on Mardi Gras day?
Do you really chase chickens when you want to play?
I've never practiced Voodoo, have you?
I want to see a crawfish, do they have them in your zoos?
How high can a brown pelican fly?
My mom said that you eat something called a meat pie.
Does a Magnolia flower smell really sweet?
I'm getting hungry, do you have any King Cake to eat?
What does it mean if I get the baby in my cake?
Does it mean good luck? 'Cause that would be great!
I can't wait to come to Louisiana again!
When I come can I bring my friends?

!

Louisiana

A Parish is a Poem

A parish is a poem.
Louisiana is my home.
You can't make gumbo without a roux.
You can't go dancin' without dancin' shoes.
A parish in a song.
With love in your heart, you can't go wrong.

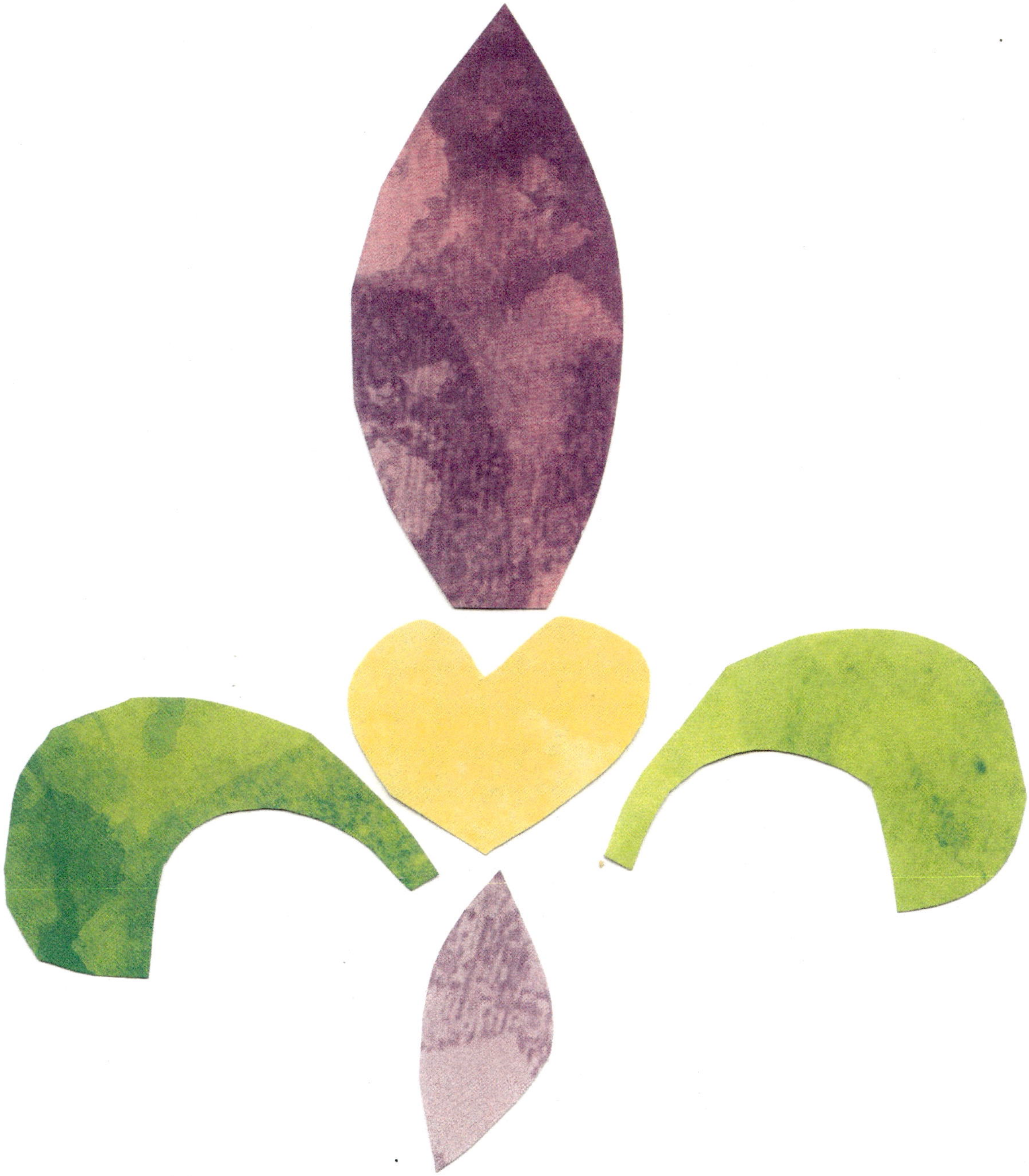

Black Eyed Peas for Dinner

Black Eyed Pea.
One Two Three.
Lemonade mix.
Four Five Six.
Mommas in the kitchen.
Seven Eight Nine.
Better be home for dinner on time.

123

Opie the Dog

Golden hair
Big brown eyes
Doggie hugs that make me smile.
One ear flops,
the other stands tall.
He's the best dog of them all.
Opie! Opie! Good little pup!
Opie! Opie! Sent from Heaven above.

Gumbo Rat

Gumbo alligator
Gumbo cat
Gumbo file'
Gumbo hat
Gumbo crawfish
Gumbo pig
Gumbo dance
Gumbo jig
Gumbo Joe
Gumbo Bob
Gumbo Sue
Gumbo Sob
Gumbo this
Gumbo that
Gumbo fish
Gumbo rat

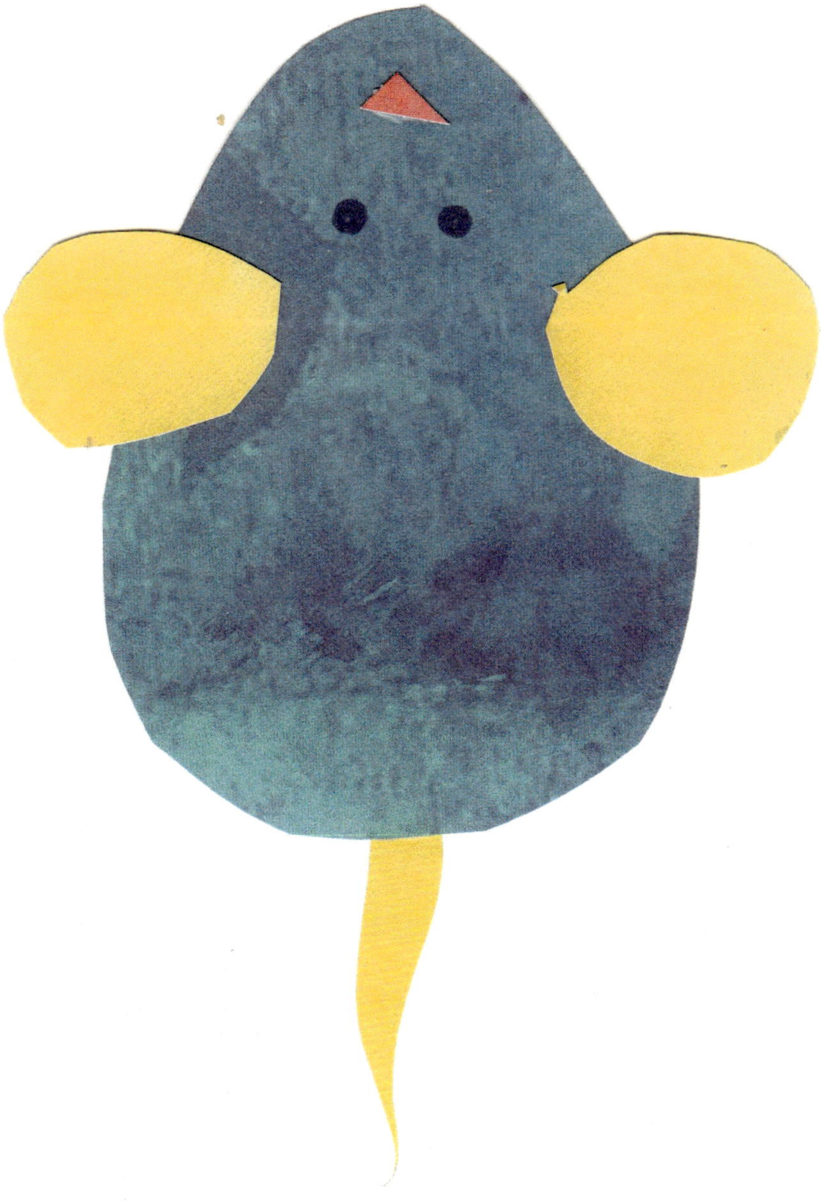

Turnip Greens

Bayou blue.
How do you do?
Baton Rouge red.
Warm cornbread.
Sunflower yellow.
Hello fella'.
Turnip Greens.
Best you ever seen.

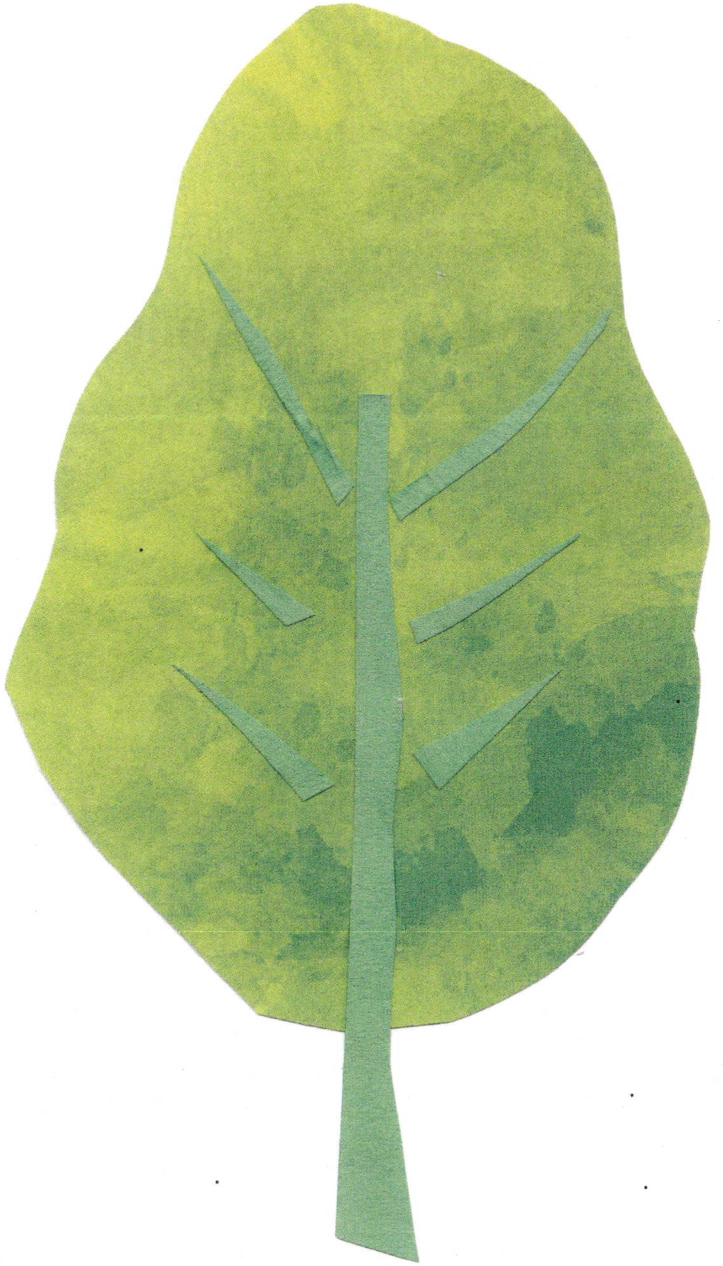

The Rougarou

Swamp.
Green water.
Grand Cypress knees.
The Rougarou lives there.
Visit him if you please.

Hide and Seek

Frog hopped.
Alligator swam.
Crawfish said, "Here I am!"
Cricket chirped.
Bird flew.
Crawfish said, "Where are you?"

WHERE ARE YOU?

Simple Life

Mud puddle in the yard
Pick up sticks
House of cards
Simple life
Simple smile
Dirt road
yonder a mile.
Tall grass
Sugar cane.
Sunday Mass.
Memory lane.
Mud puddle in the yard.
Pick up sticks
House of cards

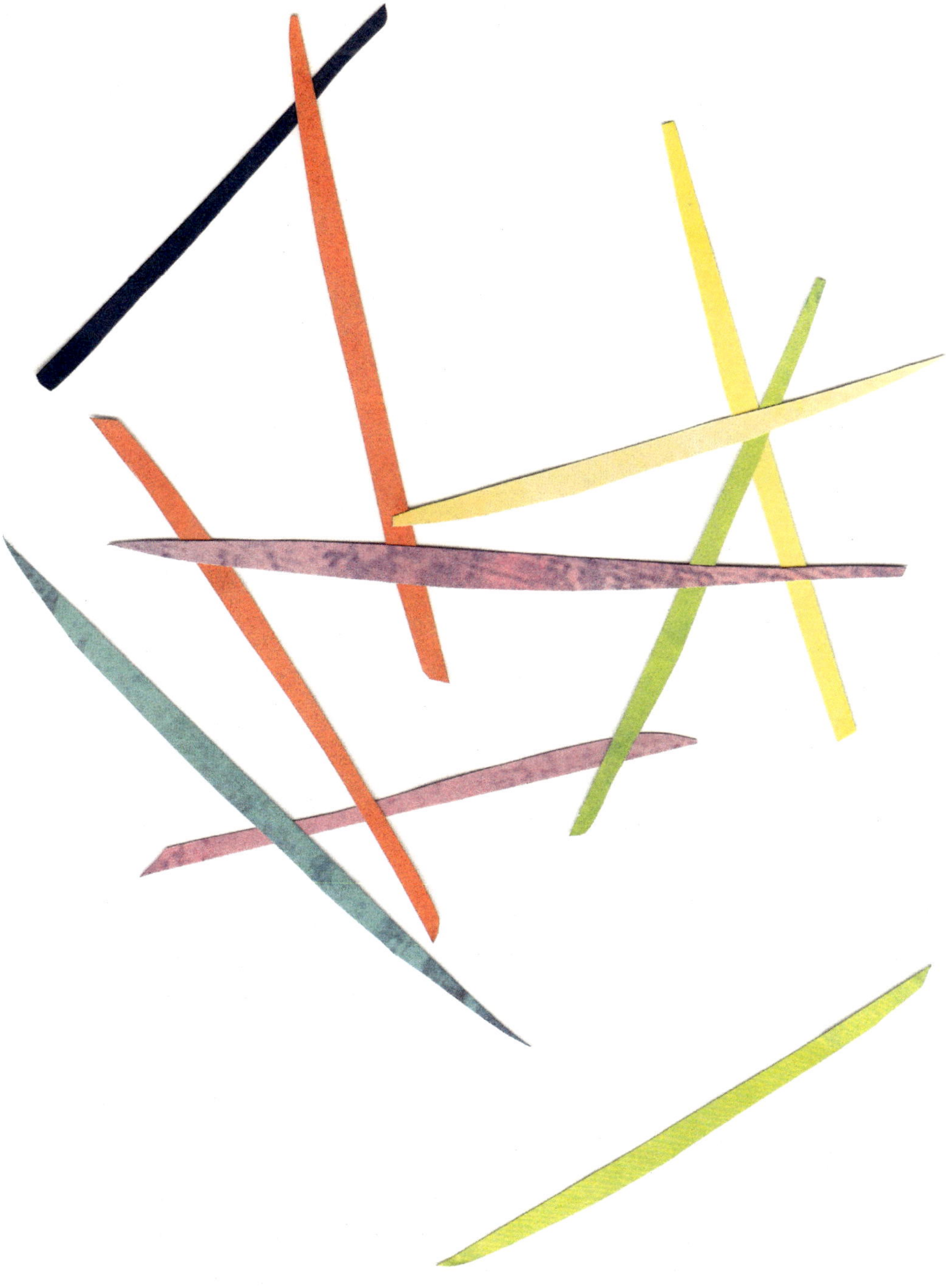

Pears and Prayers

Prayers and pears.
Moon and spoon.
Kiss me dear. I love you.
The sun was bright. The tide was high. So we thought we'd take a drive.
We saw a field of sunflowers in bloom. Our eyes gazed to Heaven to look for you.
I saw a heart up in the sky. I blew a kiss and told you "hi."
Prayers and pears.
Smiles and miles.
Where have you been? It has been a while.
The day grew long. I sang your song. I don't know how I've stayed so strong.
Prayers and pears.
Moon and spoon.
Kiss me dear. I love you.

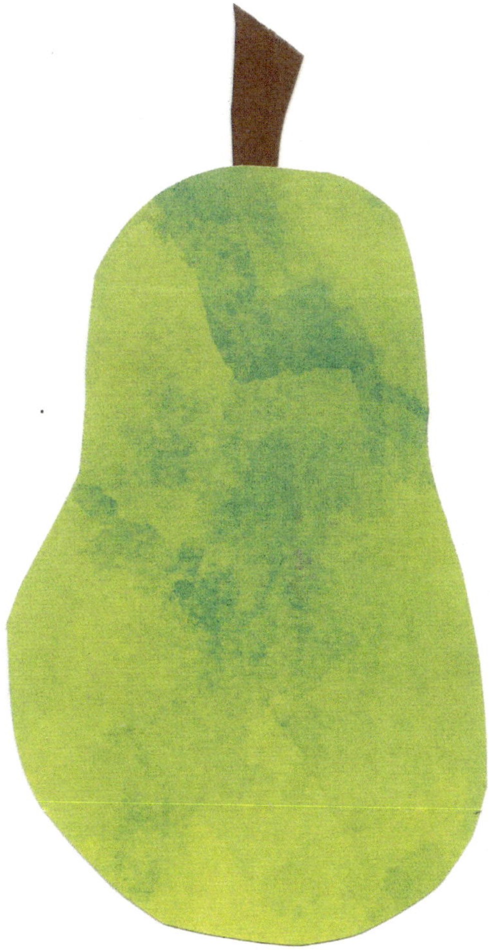

Made in the USA
Columbia, SC
20 July 2022